Hector

LIVES IN
THE UNITED STATES NOW

The Story of a Mexican-American Child

By Joan Hewett – Photographs by Richard Hewett

J. B. LIPPINCOTT · 1792 · NEW YORK

Typography by Andrew Rhodes

1 2 3 4 5 6 7 8 9 10

First Edition

Library of Congress Cataloging-in-Publication Data
Hewett, Joan.
    Hector lives in the United States now : the story of a Mexican-
American child / by Joan Hewett ; photographs by Richard Hewett.
        p.   cm.
    Includes bibliographical references.
    Summary: Text and photographs document the day-to-day happenings
and milestones in the life of a young Mexican boy whose family seeks
amnesty in the United States under the Immigration Reform and
Control Act.
    ISBN 0-397-32295-X : $. — ISBN 0-397-32278-X (lib. bdg.) : $
    1. Mexican Americans—Juvenile literature.   2. Mexican American
children—Juvenile literature.   [1. Mexican Americans.]
I. Hewett, Richard, ill.   II. Title.
E184.M5H46 1990   89-36572
973′.046872—dc20   CIP
                                                                    AC

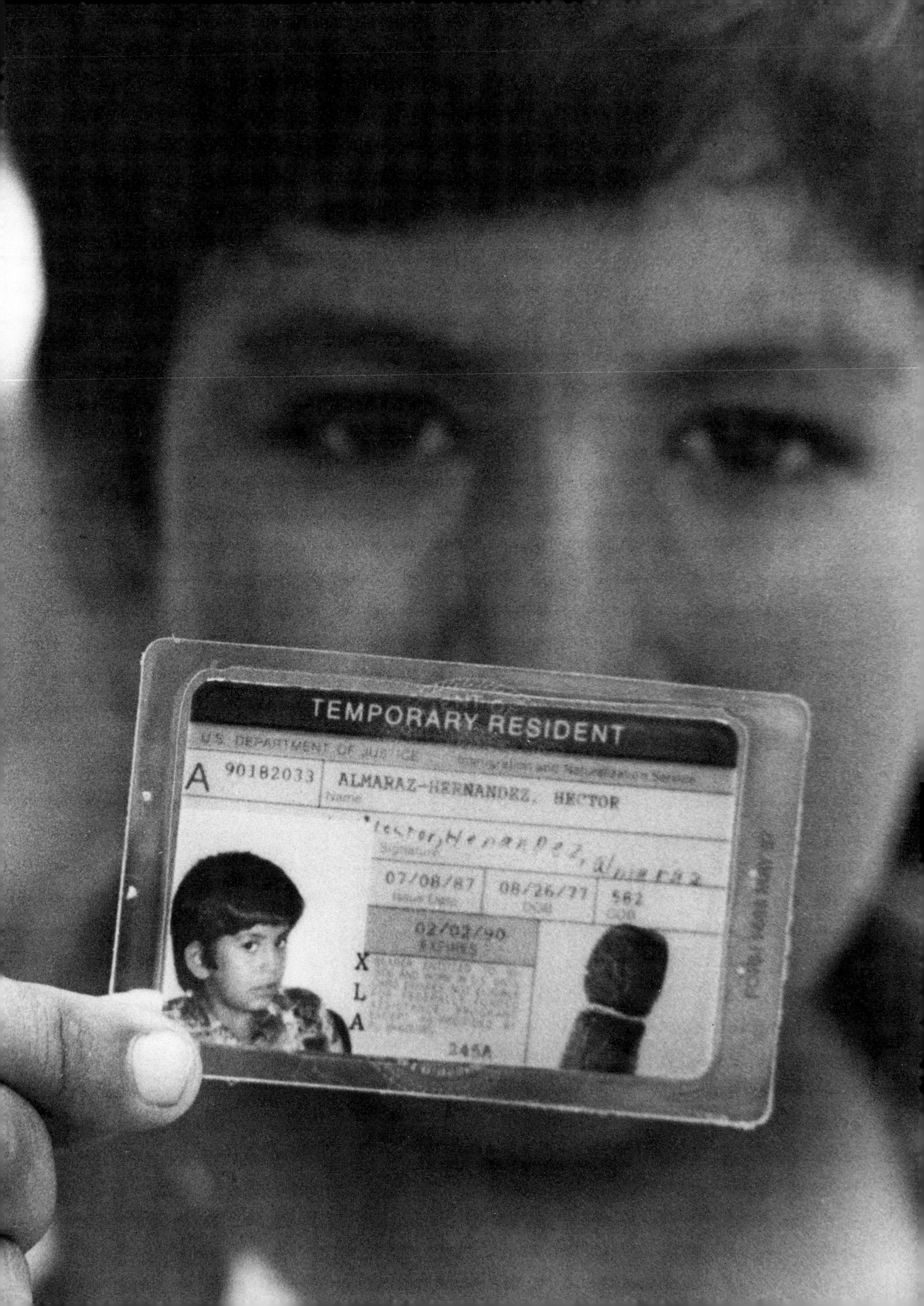
TEMPORARY RESIDENT
U.S. DEPARTMENT OF JUSTICE
A
90182033
ALMARAZ-HERNANDEZ, HECTOR
Name
07/08/87
08/26/77
582
02/02/90
EXPIRES
XLA

Ten-year-old Hector Almaraz is a Mexican American. For as long as he can remember he has lived in Los Angeles—in this neighborhood, on this block.

Hector's parents are Leopoldo and Rosario Almaraz. He also has three brothers: nine-year-old Polo, and Miguel and Ernesto, who are seven and four.

Hector and Polo were born in Guadalajara, Mexico, and are Mexican citizens, like their parents. Their younger brothers, Miguel and Ernesto, were born in Los Angeles and are American citizens.

When Hector's parents came to California to find work, they did not understand English. But they had heard so much about Los Angeles, from sisters and brothers and their own parents, that the city seemed almost familiar.

At first they stayed with relatives. Then Leopoldo found a job, and the family moved to Eagle Rock, a residential section of the city.

They are still there. The streets and parks are safe, and an elementary school and a Catholic church are only a few blocks from their small, bungalow-style apartment.

Hector has lots of friends. Most of them live on his block. They play together after school and on Saturdays and Sundays.

Soccer is one of their favorite games. So is baseball. When it is baseball season, they dig out a bat, ball, and glove and practice batting in a backyard or alley. Other times they go to the park to play volleyball, or just to see what is going on. If no one has a flat, they ride their bikes over; otherwise they walk.

Like his friends, Hector likes to read comic books and collect baseball cards. Sometimes they gather their cards or books, meet on the front stoop, and trade. Although the children talk and joke in English, their parents come from Mexico and Central America, and Spanish is the language spoken in their homes.

When Hector and Polo are drawing or doing their homework at the kitchen table, they often tell stories to each other in English. They speak as fast as they can so their mother will not understand them. Rosario gets annoyed because she suspects they do it just to tease her.

Although Hector and Polo speak English equally well, their parents think it proper that their eldest boy be the family spokesperson. Hector enjoys the responsibility. Whenever someone who can only speak English telephones them, Hector is called to the phone. Or when Rosario has to get a prescription filled at the drugstore, Hector goes along to talk to the pharmacist.

Hector did not speak English when he started kindergarten. It was a scary time. He was away from his mother and brothers. He understood only a few English words and did not know what was going on in class. In first grade Hector had trouble learning to read. But he was determined to learn English, and by the end of the second grade he was reading and writing as well as his classmates. School started to be fun.

Now Hector is a fifth grader, one of the big kids. In United States history, his class is reading about the different immigrant groups who helped settle the West. Their teacher says, "We are a nation of immigrants. Indians, also called Native Americans, have lived here for thousands of years. Everyone else has come to the continental United States from some other place." Then she smiles and says, "Let's find out about us."

The students in Hector's class are told to ask their parents about their ancestors and then write a brief history of their families. It is an exciting project. When they finish their reports, they will glue snapshots of themselves to their papers and hang them on the wall. But first they get to read them aloud.

Philip traces his family back as far as his great-great-great-grandmother. His ancestors lived on a small Philippine island. Many of them were fishermen. Philip, his sister, and his parents are the only people in his family who have settled in the United States.

One side of Nicky's family came from Norway and Germany. His other ancestors came from Ireland and Sweden. All of them were farmers, and when they came to this country they homesteaded land, which means they farmed and built a house on uncultivated public land that then became theirs under a special homestead law.

Vanessa's great-great-grandmother was a Yaqui Indian from Sonora, Mexico. Her grandfather fought in the Mexican Revolution. Another one of her ancestors was French.

Erick is descended from Ukrainian, German, and Italian immigrants. His German grandfather and Ukrainian grandmother met in a prisoner-of-war camp. When they were released, they married and came to the United States by ship.

Julie is of French, Irish, and Spanish descent. Her Great-Great-Grandma Elm was born in Texas. When Elm was a child her family moved to California. They traveled by covered wagon.

Everyone is interested in Kyria's family history. One of her African ancestors was a soldier in the American Revolution. Another fought for the Confederacy in the Civil War. Other members of her family homesteaded in Oklahoma.

Hector tells the class about his Mexican ancestors. They were farmers and carpenters.

There are twelve other Mexican-American children in Hector's class, and some two hundred fifty thousand Mexican-American students in Los Angeles schools.

Before California became part of the United States, it belonged to Mexico. Some Mexican families have lived in California for hundreds of years, but most Mexican-American children are recent arrivals. Their numbers will keep increasing.

Compared to the United States, Mexico is not a prosperous country, and in the last few years Mexico's economy has declined sharply. More than half its workers cannot find jobs. So, many go north to look for jobs on the other side of the Mexican-American border, a 1,900-mile boundary that separates California, Arizona, New Mexico, and Texas from Mexico.

Some Mexicans are among the six hundred thousand immigrants from all over the world who are granted permanent residence in the United States each year. Other Mexican workers and their families enter this country with temporary work cards, and still others cross the border illegally, without documents. Many have lived in the United States for a long time.

Now, under the amnesty provision of a new immigration law, a large number of these people can become permanent legal residents and, eventually, citizens. To qualify, an immigrant must have entered the United States before 1982 and have lived here continuously for five or more years.

Hector's parents qualify easily because they have been living in this country since 1980. But even though their temporary work cards had expired some time ago, at first they were not sure they wanted to apply for amnesty and become citizens. They feared that they might always feel like outsiders here. The stylishly groomed men and women who go to work in business suits, own their own homes, and speak English without an accent seem to live in a world quite different from their own.

Leopoldo works hard. Each weekday, while his children are still asleep, he leaves for his job at a run-down factory in the city's garment district. He repairs and maintains the machinery. Except for Leopoldo's boss, everyone who works in the factory is a Spanish-speaking immigrant. Leopoldo doubts that anyone really wants to work there, but it is the best job he could get and he is glad to have it. He is pleased that he has been able to buy his family a color TV, a VCR, a van that is only a few years old, a radio with stereophonic sound, and their own telephone. He is also proud that he makes enough money so his wife does not have to work.

Rosario did work until Miguel was born. Now she keeps the family's one-bedroom apartment clean and orderly, does the shopping, cooks, manages the family's money, and makes sure that Hector, Polo, and Miguel do well in school. In Guadalajara there was no need for Rosario to drive, and she still has not learned how. But her girl friend drives, and they do everything together. Rosario brings Ernesto, and her friend brings her little girl. Their weekly trip to the Laundromat never seems like work, and every so often they go to the Eagle Rock Mall, take the escalator from one level to another, look at all the latest fashions, and try on earrings.

Some of Leopoldo's and Rosario's sisters and brothers live nearby. The families get together on birthdays and holidays and enjoy putting up Christmas trees, having parties with fancy store-bought cakes and piñatas stuffed with candy, making colorful Easter baskets, and barbecuing *carne asada* and other treats while picnicking in a local park.

But even though Leopoldo and Rosario are not lonely, they miss Mexico. It seems like home. They planned to return once their four children were grown and on their own. Everything costs far less in Mexico. With their savings they could buy a fine house in Guadalajara, and be respected members of the community in which they were raised.

Despite this dream, Leopoldo and Rosario decided to apply for amnesty. They believe that their children's future lies in the United States and think amnesty might be Hector and Polo's only chance to become American citizens.

Now Leopoldo, Rosario, Hector, and Polo have received temporary legal-resident cards. The amnesty period will end in a couple of months, and special classes in English and United States history and government will be offered so people can qualify for their permanent papers. But Leopoldo wanted to start studying before then. He has been attending an English-as-a-second-language class four nights a week at a local high school, and Rosario has been learning English at a nearby church so she can keep up with her children and help them with their homework.

Hector is proud of his new official status. His card is kept in a safe place with the family's other important documents. But Hector was permitted to carry it with him when the whole family drove to Tijuana, a Mexican city right over the border. They went because they were free to! United States customs officers could no longer prevent the Almaraz family from coming back. While they were there, they ate tacos and *raspados*, Mexican snow cones, and wandered in and out of shops to look for new suits for Hector and Polo. Their first communion is just a few weeks away.

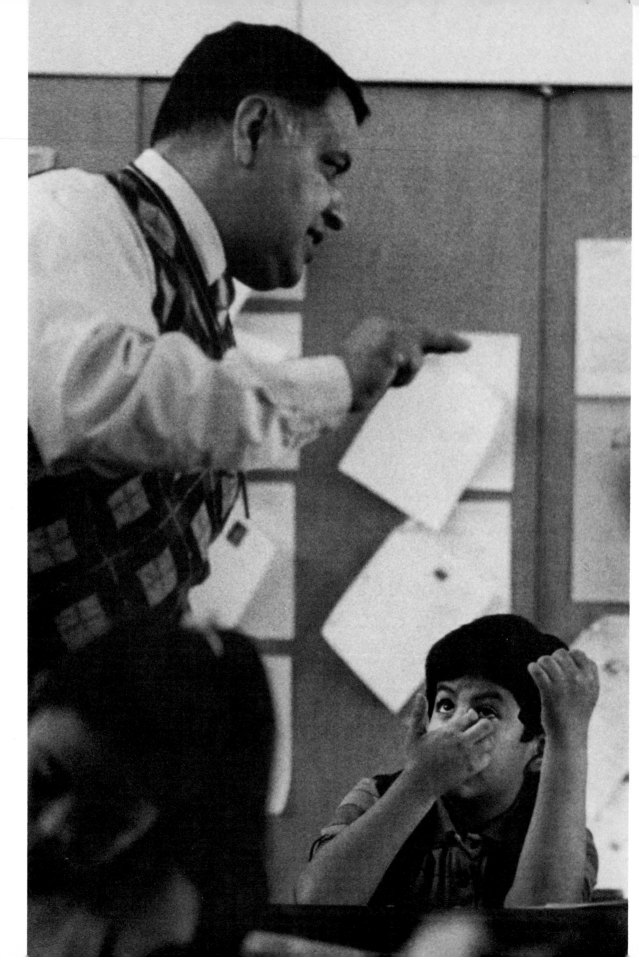

Hector and Polo have been taking catechism classes on Saturdays for nearly two years to prepare them for their first communion. So have their friends Eduardo and Vidal, two brothers who live in the same bungalow court. The four boys ride their bikes to Saint Dominic's, a local Catholic school. There are several Saturday catechism classes. Hector and Eduardo are in the same one. When all the children are there they form a circle, hold hands, and say a prayer. Sometimes it is a formal prayer; sometimes the catechist, or instructor, asks one of the children to make one up.

During each class the catechist asks a series of questions about basic church doctrine. The children answer in chorus.

"Who are we?" "We are the children of God."

"Who is in you?" "The Holy Spirit."

The children also read and discuss Bible stories or folk tales. One Saturday they read a tale about villagers who each gave the few vegetables they had to make soup for everyone and through sharing became "strangers no more."

The following Saturday the catechist brings carrots, celery, canned soup, and an electric burner. They cook and eat the food and talk about sharing and loving.

Most of Hector's classmates at Saint Dominic's will receive communion at one of the church's English-language masses. But Hector and Polo, and some of the other Spanish-speaking children, will receive communion at the Spanish-language mass, the one the Almaraz family usually goes to.

A note from Saint Dominic's arrives with information about first communion. Hector listens as his mother telephones uncles and aunts and lets them know when they should be at the church or what they might bring to the picnic they will have afterward. He writes, in Spanish, to his cousin Guadalupe in Guadalajara. Of all his cousins, thirteen-year-old Guadalupe is closest to him in age. They have written back and forth a couple of times. Now Hector tells his cousin all about his upcoming first communion.

Before the boys go to sleep, Rosario reads Bible stories to them in Spanish from books that she brought from Mexico. After a while Hector and Polo take turns reading.

In school, the teacher hands back the nutrition test the class took two days ago. Hector is pleased. Despite a few punctuation mistakes, he got an A⁻. He rewrites the sentences that had mistakes, putting commas and periods in the right places. Then it is time for recess, math, and lunch.

Hector lines up with his friends outside the cafeteria. They get their food and find a table. The girls at the opposite end of the table ignore them, and they ignore the girls. Soon they are talking about roller coasters: which is the fastest, which is the scariest.... Hector's favorite amusement park is Magic Mountain, and his absolutely favorite attraction is the Revolution, because you ride it upside down!

The first-communion rehearsal is that night. In Hispanic cultures, the *padrinos*, or godparents, play an important role in a child's upbringing and take part in First Holy Communion. Alex, who is married to one of Rosario's sisters, is Hector's godfather. Pancho, one of Leopoldo's brothers, is Polo's. They attend the rehearsal with the boys and listen carefully to what the boys have learned.

Saturday morning seems like a holiday. There are no catechism classes. Hector and Polo watch cartoons until they are bored, then they go to the park with their friends. When they get back, the rich, tangy smell of chili greets them. In the kitchen Rosario kneads tortilla dough that she has made from corn flour and water. Then she forms it into

tortillas, cooks them on a special griddle, and fills them with steaming chili. Her chili tacos are a family favorite and they have them every weekend. And every weekend night, the Almarazes gather around their TV set. They watch their favorite shows and play videos that Leopoldo has rented. The spookier a movie is, the more they enjoy it.

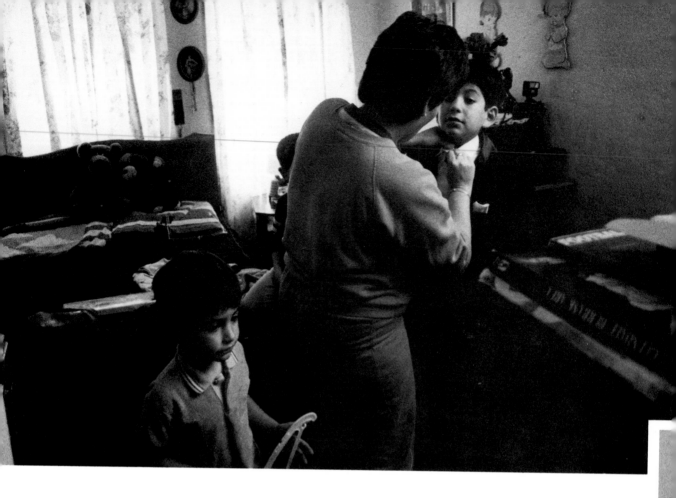

On Sunday, Hector wakes up at dawn. He lies still and thinks.... After today, after he receives communion, he won't be a little kid anymore. His mama and papa will no longer be responsible for him spiritually. He will be responsible for himself.... He turns over. Polo is awake also.

Soon everyone is up, and the house is a hub of activity.

A tailor by trade, Leopoldo bends over the sewing machine, finishing the second shirt for the boys. After they priced dress shirts for communion, he decided to make them himself. Rosario irons Leopoldo's slacks and her dress. She tells Miguel and Ernesto they can play inside, but not outside. The TV set blares. Leopoldo's youngest brother, Listen, arrives. He has volunteered to blow dry and style Hector's and Polo's hair.

Their friend Vidal knocks on the front door. Like Hector and Polo, he is wearing a black suit, white shirt, and black tie. Following a Hispanic custom, each boy will get a white bow from his godparent to wear on his arm.

Now the three boys inspect themselves in the mirror. Some neighborhood friends gather outside. They want to come in and see how Hector, Polo, and Vidal look.

Finally it is time to leave. Hector feels excited, nervous, and a little strange as they step out into the sun and walk toward the church. When they reach the church courtyard, he is relieved that his godfather and Polo's are already there.

The children line up. The catechism director makes sure that every communicant has a candle. Moments later they are marching down the aisle.

Each boy and girl sits with his or her family. Violins and guitars play, the children sing hymns, and everyone joins hands and says the Lord's Prayer. Father Rodolfo, the priest, talks about the meaning of this special day. Then, before the children receive the bread and sip the wine of their first communion, each child walks up to the altar with his

godparents or parents. On the altar a big candle burns, symbolizing the "light of Christ." Hector's and Polo's godparents take the boys' candles and light them from the big altar candle.

When the mass is over Hector feels happy and proud. The Almaraz family goes off to a picnic with other Hispanic families whose children have received Holy Communion for the first time. It seems like a fiesta. Hector and Polo race to see who will reach the merry-go-round first.

On Monday, still feeling happy and proud, Hector leaves for school extra early. Although Hector does not look forward to school all the time, when he is there he enjoys it. He likes to learn new things, and he likes to do them well. Besides, at recess and lunch he has fun with his friends.

Hector always tries to complete his homework during study period. When he can't, he finishes it at home. Hector's parents had only a grade school education, and his grandparents did not go to school at all. Hector knows that he is the first one in his family to have the chance to go on to high school, and he does not intend to let his family down.

Hector does not know yet what he wants to do after high school, but computers intrigue him, and he wonders if he might like working with them.

A few months ago he took a short beginner's computer lesson so that he could use the computers at his local public library. The library has computer games, and for a while he had great fun playing them. Then they seemed too simple. But he read a book about the different kinds of things computers can do and is looking forward to taking a real computer course when he's a little older.

Before Hector started using the library's computers he had only been to the library once, on a trip with his whole class. Now it is a place he visits regularly. Polo and Victor, one of his neighborhood friends, go with him. They take out books on building kites and drawing dinosaurs. And after watching TV dramas about John F. Kennedy, Robert Kennedy, and Martin Luther King, Jr., Hector read books about them.

Because Hector is curious about past events and famous public figures, his parents gave him a thick, hardcover book about the last one hundred years of United States history. When no one is leafing through it, the book sits on a special shelf beside an English dictionary. Aside from the dictionary, it is the first English-language book Hector's family has purchased.

Now it is May 2, 1988. May 4th marks the closing of amnesty. The radio announcer on Hector's mother's favorite Mexican music station keeps reminding listeners that they have only three more days to apply for amnesty. So far one and a half million people have filled out applications. Surveys show that there are six million or more undocumented immigrants. No one knows how many of those people might be eligible.

Sometimes Hector wonders why people should need a special document to live where they want to live, or go where they want to go. But he is happy to know that he can leave the United States anytime and not be barred from coming back. Hector has a friend who has just become a legal resident and will be visiting his relatives in Mexico this summer. Like Hector, he is from Guadalajara and left at such an early age that he cannot remember what it was like.

One Saturday Leopoldo and Rosario announce that the whole family will be going to Guadalajara. Not this summer, because Leopoldo can't get off from work then. They will be going over Christmas vacation!

Hector is thrilled. He will see his grandparents and his aunts and uncles. He will be with Guadalupe, the cousin he has been writing to. His papa says they will take their van or go by bus. Either way, they will get to really see Mexico. And either way, he will get out of school two weeks early.

Leopoldo and Rosario talk about how happy they will be to see everyone. Starting Friday they will begin saving a little money each week so they can buy Christmas presents for everyone they will visit in Mexico. The boys want to know more about the trip.

Finally they run out of questions. Leopoldo leaves for the video store, taking Polo and Miguel with him. Rosario starts to make chili. Ernesto goes outside to play. And Hector and his friends head for the park.

AUTHORS' NOTE

The Immigration Reform and Control Act, enacted in November 1986, provided amnesty for undocumented aliens who could prove they had continuously lived in the United States since January 1, 1982. The one-year amnesty period ended in May 1988. One million six hundred thousand aliens were granted legal residence and the opportunity to become American citizens. Included were people from around the world, but the largest number, by far, were from Mexico.

FURTHER READING

•

If you would like to read about Mexican history and culture, or if you would like to find out about other Mexican Americans and their experiences, or learn about other Hispanic-American groups who have come and are still coming to this country, there are many excellent books to choose from. They differ widely. Biography, story book, history, myth, photo documentary and mystery, here are a few that might interest you.

Brenner, Barbara. *Mystery of the Plumed Serpent*. New York: Knopf, 1981. Twins who live in New York City learn about pre-Columbian history and legends as they solve a mystery.

•

Garver, Susan, and McGuire, Paula. *Coming to North America: From Mexico, Cuba and Puerto Rico*. New York: Delacorte, 1981. Explores the Hispanic immigrant experience.

•

Hewett, Joan. *Getting Elected: The Diary of a Campaign*. Illustrated by Richard Hewett. New York: Lodestar, 1989. Gloria Molina, California's first Mexican-American state assemblywoman, runs for city council. A photo essay.

•

Hinojosa, Francisco. *The Old Lady Who Ate People: Frightening Stories*. Illustrated by Leonel Maciel. Boston: Little, Brown, 1984. Four Mexican legends of spirits and phantoms, with appropriately scary illustrations by an outstanding Mexican artist.

•

Kurtycz, Marcos, and Kobeh, Ana Garcia. *Tigers and Opossums: Animal Legends*. Boston: Little, Brown, 1984. From the days of old Mexican Indian tribes, animal fables with vivid artistic drawings. Good for group storytelling.

•

Meltzer, Milton. *The Hispanic Americans*. New York: Crowell, 1982. Discusses the social and economic problems faced by Hispanic Americans who live and work in the United States today.

•

Politi, Leo. *Three Stalks of Corn*. New York: Scribner's, 1976. Angelica's grandmother explains the importance of corn in the life and legends of the Mexican people. Full-color illustrations.

•

Roberts, Naurice. *Henry Cisneros, Mexican-American Mayor*. Chicago: Children's Press, 1986. A brief but concise biography of the young Mexican-American mayor of San Antonio, Texas.

Smith, Eileen L. *Mexico: Giant of the South*. Minneapolis: Dillon, 1983. An overview of Mexico's history and customs, with emphasis on the twentieth century.

•

White, Florence M. *Cesar Chavez: Man of Courage*. Champaign, Ill.: Garrard Publishing Co., 1973. How Chavez, against impossible odds, organized the first successful farm workers' union in the United States.

•

Wolf, Bernard. *In This Proud Land*. New York: Lippincott, 1978. Portrait, in words and photographs, of a Mexican-American migrant farm family.

ACKNOWLEDGMENTS

We are most grateful to Carlos Barrón, Director, Mexican American Education Commission, Los Angeles Unified School District, and Father Rodolfo Vega, O. P., Associate, Saint Dominic Church, for their interest and valuable input. For their splendid cooperation we thank: Betty Palmer, Bernice Hallam, and the staff and students of Eagle Rock Elementary; Maria Velasquez and Tony Rosales, Saint Dominic Church, Religious Education; Saeed Ali, Division Chairman, English as a Second Language Classes, Glendale Community College; George Milner, Jr., Pastor, Eagle Rock Lutheran Church; Los Angeles Public Library librarians Renny Day, Children's Literature, and Janet Woo, Children's Services; and the Almaraz family's many relatives and friends. And a deeply felt thanks to Leopoldo and Rosario Almaraz and their children, Hector, Polo, Miguel, and Ernesto, for opening their home to us and making this book possible.

Thanks also go to Linda Zuckerman Knab for suggesting the idea, and Robert O. Warren for his fine editing.